W9-BZU-354

First edition for the United States and Canada published
in 2010 by Barron's Educational Series, Inc.

First edition of *I can do it!*
first published in 2010 by Wayland, a division of Hachette Children's Books

All inquiries should be addressed to:
Barron's Educational Series, Inc.
250 Wireless Boulevard
Hauppauge, NY 11788
www.barronseduc.com

Library of Congress Control No.: 2010923339

ISBN-13: 978-0-7641-4515-5
ISBN-10: 0-7641-4515-0

Printed in China
9 8 7 6 5 4 3 2 1

Manufactured by: Shenzhen Wing King Tong Paper Products Co. Ltd., Shenzhen, Guangdong, China.
May 2010

I can do it!

A FIRST LOOK AT NOT GIVING UP

PAT THOMAS
ILLUSTRATED BY LESLEY HARKER

BARRON'S

Have you ever tried
to do something that
was really hard?

It was so hard that you felt like you wanted to give up?

People enjoy doing things that are easy,
and that they are good at.

Sometimes it's hard to understand why you should keep trying to do something that seems quite hard at first.

9

Learning to do new things makes
life more interesting.

It also makes us more interesting people to be
around and more able to help and take part
in the things going on around us.

But learning anything new often takes patience
and practice—even for grown-ups.

What about you?

Can you think of some things you've tried that have been hard?

Did you give up or did you keep trying?

Whether you are learning a new sport or how to play an instrument, or doing a math problem or a puzzle, or trying to figure out how to play a new game...

...if you want to get better at it, you need to be stubborn and keep at it. To keep trying is how you learn to do something hard.

Most of us don't get things right—
or do them well—the first time we try.

When you don't get something right the
first time it's normal to feel frustrated
and sad and angry.

But don't let that stop you from
trying again.

Thinking that you can't do it can make getting it right even harder.

So always try to tell yourself,
"I can do it."

And listen to others when they
encourage you and tell you that
they believe in you, too.

Remember, it's not so
important to always
win or be the best.

It's more important to
always do your best and to
finish what you have started.

No matter what you are doing,
when you know you have tried your best,
then you can be really proud of yourself.

And your friends and family
will be proud of you, too.

What about you?

Do you think it is always important to win? How does it feel when
you can't do something well? Can you think of some times when
you didn't win, but you felt proud that you tried really hard?

Some people only ever do the things
they know they will be good at.

They never try anything
new because they are afraid they might fail.

Or they are afraid that
people might make
fun of them.

Or they might let their friends and families down.

But trying new things is part of life.

It teaches you new skills, helps you to find new ways of solving problems and gives you confidence.

Life would be pretty boring if we
only ever did the things that were easy,
or played the games we knew we could.

So try not to be afraid
of things that seem
hard at first.

With a little effort you may just find they are the things you enjoy doing the most.

HOW TO USE THIS BOOK

This book provides a basic introduction to the concept of perseverance. Perseverance is the ability to keep trying to learn something new or to do something better. It takes working hard when it feels easier to quit. It takes not giving in to disappointment, discouragement, or frustration. Perseverance strengthens people's willpower even if they don't get what they want, because they don't give up. You can reinforce this message by providing day to day lessons in perseverance for your child. When you teach your children to persevere you are giving them an important practical and emotional skill that will help them throughout their lives. While some children find it easier to stick with things, all can learn some aspects of this trait.

As with any new skill, it's important to make the lesson fun and age appropriate. Young children can be encouraged to finish or complete a craft project or persevere with a puzzle. Small achievable goals can produce a big sense of accomplishment. As your child gets older let him or her lead in deciding what to achieve next—whether it's learning to skate or swim or just getting to the top of the monkey bars—and let your child go at his or her own pace. Instead of jumping in immediately when your child is struggling, try to cheer from the sidelines. Letting your child know that you have faith in his or her ability to figure things out can boost self-esteem and provide the encouragement needed to finish things.

Children learn by example, so make sure you include your child in your own goal-setting behavior. Adults understand how to break down complex tasks and goals into smaller steps, and showing how this process works passes an important skill on to your child. Be aware of family language as well, as how it can reinforce defeatism. Phrases like "I can't..." and "I'll never..." can make everyone feel like giving up. Saying "I know I can do it!" and "I don't want to give up," and even truisms like "Winners never quit, quitters never win," and "If at first you don't succeed, try, try again!" help keep a positive frame of mind.

At the same time keep an eye on the bigger picture of why you might want your child to persevere. Is it because you want your child to be the "best" in comparison to others, to win medals and external praise, or to do his or her "best" and feel a sense of personal achievement? Be aware also of asking children to persevere with things that clearly make them unhappy. When your child does persevere, show that you're proud of his or her commitment, effort, and determination above and beyond any trophy, grade, or medal they might get.

In the classroom teachers can lead discussions on what perseverance means and does not mean. For example: keep working until the assignment is complete instead of trying only a few times and quitting. With the help of students, list the steps that are needed to learn a new skill such as riding a bicycle, learning to swim, or memorizing times tables. Students can also write or draw a picture illustrating a time when they persevered and succeeded even though they felt like giving up, and then discuss the feelings associated with their achievement.

Stories about perseverance can provide good topics for reports and discussions, as do biographies of real-life people such as Albert Einstein, Helen Keller, Thomas Edison, Mother Teresa, and Madame (Marie) Curie. School visits and talks from a respected community member who overcame obstacles can make the lesson more "real."

BOOKS TO READ

Never Give Up: Learning About Perseverance
Regina Burch (Creative Teaching Press, 2002)

Dog Tired: A Learning Adventure in Perseverance
Tony Salerno (New Leaf Press, 2005)

Horton Hatches the Egg
Dr. Seuss (HarperCollins Children's Books, 2004)

The Little Engine That Could
Watty Piper (G. P. Putnam's Sons, 2002)

The Very Busy Spider
Eric Carle (Grosset & Dunlap, 2006)

Stuart Little
E. B. White (Puffin, 2007)

The Children's Book of Virtues
William J. Bennett (Simon & Schuster, 1996)

Keep Trying, Travis!
Jodee McConnaughhay (Standard Publishing, 2005)

Keep Trying Little Zebra
Christina Wilsdon (Readers Digest Young Families, 2004)

RESOURCES FOR ADULTS

The Values Book: Teaching Sixteen Basic Values to Young Children
Pam Schiller, Tamera Bryant (Gryphon House, 1998)

Teaching Your Children Values
Linda and Richard Eyre (Fireside, 1993)

The Book of Virtues: A Treasury of Great Moral Stories
William J. Bennett (Simon & Schuster, 1993)

What Do You Stand For?
Barbara A. Lewis (Free Spirit, 1998)